IN BUSINESS NOW

Retailing

Peter Jones
and
Steve Baron

First edition 1991

Published by
MACMILLAN EDUCATION LTD
Houndmills, Basingstoke, Hampshire RG21 2XS
and London
Companies and representatives
throughout the world

Filmset by Wearside Tradespools, Fulwell, Sunderland

Printed in Hong Kong

British Library Cataloguing in Publication Data
Jones, Peter
Retailing. – (In business now)
I. Title II. Baron, Steve III. Series
381
ISBN 0–333–54447–1

In Business Now Series
Ethics Francis McHugh
Graphs and Charts Renée Huggett
Markets Renée Huggett
Retailing Peter Jones and Steve Baron

Contents

Acknowledgements iv

1 Retailing 1
2 Buying 7
3 Quality Control 10
4 Physical Distribution Management 14
5 Merchandising 18
6 Selling 22
7 Management and Control 27
8 Retail Strategy 32
9 Market Research 37
10 Consumer Behaviour 40
11 Marketing and Advertising 43
12 Electronic Technology 47
13 Customer Service 51
14 Human Resources and People Skills 55
15 Retailing in the Future 58

Index 63

Acknowledgements

The authors and publishers thank GR Photography for providing the photographs included in this book. Other illustrative material is acknowledged individually where it appears in the text.

The authors would like to thank Jenny who typed an often obscure manuscript, their colleagues in the Department of Retail Marketing at Manchester Polytechnic for their support, and the former landlord of the 'Coach and Horses' on London Road who provided liquid refreshment.

Unit 1 Retailing

Introduction

Britain has been described as a nation of shopkeepers. Retailing affects all our lives and it is very big business. Let's look at a few facts and figures about retailing in the UK.

Retail turnover in 1986 was £94,000 million. In 1986 there were 250,000 retail businesses. The retail industry employs just over 2 million people (10% of the UK workforce) and an additional 1 million are employed in the related hotel and catering industry.

The top 100 UK companies (ranked by sales) contain 17 retail organisations including such well-known names as J. Sainsbury, Marks & Spencer, Tesco, Asda, Boots, Dixons and W. H. Smith. Many retailers have been very successful. Of the top 200 richest people in Britain, 53 are retailers. This includes Lord Sainsbury (J. Sainsbury) and Sir John Moores (Littlewoods), both of whom are in the top 5. Although based in the UK, a number of the large retail companies have interests in Europe, USA and the Far East (see Figure 1.1).

Retailing occurs in many shapes, sizes and forms, and ranges from small corner shops to the Metro Centre at Gateshead with 2 million sq. ft of shopping space.

Photo 1.1

Highlights of results for year ending March 1989

		£ million
Group turnover		5121.5
Group trading profit		567.4
Group operating profit		563.7
Group turnover:	UK and Eire	4454.6
	Europe	98.2
	North America and Far East	458.4
	Direct export sales outside the Group	45.8
	Financial activities	64.5
		5121.5

Figure 1.1
Marks and Spencer Group

Case Study: Metro Centre

The Metro Centre has been developed on a formerly derelict site on the outskirts of Gateshead and its 2 million sq. ft of floorspace – making it the largest enclosed shopping centre outside North America – attracts 16 million shoppers each year. The Centre contains a mixture of large stores – Marks and Spencer, House of Fraser, British Home Stores, a hypermarket – a wide range of smaller shops including River Island, Superdrug and Dixons, a fast food court, banks and building societies, a 10 screen multiplex cinema and a children's fantasy-land leisure complex. Air-conditioning, spacious shopping malls and courtyards, glazed roofs to allow the passage of natural light and water features and flowering plants are all designed to create an attractive and modern shopping and leisure environment.

What do you think are the advantages of this kind of Centre for the customer?

What are the disadvantages?

We can classify this complex industry by looking at the variety of ways and places in which retailing occurs and the different methods by which retail businesses are managed and controlled.

The Variety of Retailing

Retailing takes place in a wide range of outlets and ways including:

Department Stores – A store with a sales area of over 25,000 sq. ft, selling mainly non-food merchandise and at least 5 major lines in different departments. House of Fraser and Debenhams are well-known department stores.

Supermarket	– A self-service grocery store with a sales area of 5,000–10,000 sq. ft.
Superstores and Hypermarkets	– Superstores have a sales area of 25,000–50,000 sq. ft, selling both food and non-food goods via a self-service format. The term 'hypermarket' is usually reserved for very large superstores with well over 50,000 sq. ft of selling space and substantial car-parking facilities.
Speciality Store	– A shop specialising in the sale of a specific range of goods etc., such as Mothercare, River Island, Our Price and Dixons.
Retail Warehouse	– Retail outlets selling non-food goods – particularly furniture, carpets, toys, electrical goods and DIY – and occupying a warehouse-type building and having their own parking facilities.
Convenience Store	– Small self-service shops which serve everyday customer needs. Such shops open 7 days a week, have long opening hours and sell groceries; fresh foods; beer, wines and spirits; and basic household items.
Mail Order	– A system of retailing in which customers are offered goods in a catalogue, newspaper or directly by mail, and which are ordered by post or telephone.
Markets	– Permanent market halls with a number of regular stall-holders and more open occasional markets are one of the oldest forms of retailing.
Retailing Services	– Retailers of financial services – banks, building societies, estate agents, insurance companies – and other services such as travel agents, hairdressers, drycleaners, public houses and restaurants.

Management And Control

There are 6 main ways in which retailing is managed and controlled, namely:

1. Independent Traders – Shopkeepers running a single store.
2. Multiple Retailers – A retailer (corporate chain) operating from a number of outlets.
3. Consumer Co-operatives – A retail firm owned by its customers.
4. Contractual Chain – A group of independent retailers who engage in group buying, advertising and marketing strategies. Spar and Mace are examples.
5. Franchising – The granting of exclusive selling rights within a particular trading area. Major franchising operators include Kentucky Fried Chicken, Prontaprint and Tie Rack.
6. State-ownership – Government-owned retail outlets such as the NAAFI, which supplies goods to the Forces.

Large multiple retailers (with 10 or more outlets), such as Boots, Marks and Spencer and W. H. Smith, now dominate Britain's high streets, because they have consistently increased their share of retail trade (see Figure 1.2).

Figure 1.2
Retail trade by form of organisation, 1980–1986

	% of total retail turnover		
	1980	*1984*	*1986*
Single outlet	31.6	30.2	28.5
Small multiple (2–9 outlets)	14.6	12.6	12.3
Large multiple	53.8	57.4	59.2

Conclusion

While this chapter clearly outlines some of the variety of retail businesses, we can identify a number of basic elements that are common to most forms of retail activity. These elements are illustrated in Figure 1.3.

It is difficult to define 'retailing' but we have found the following definition most appropriate.

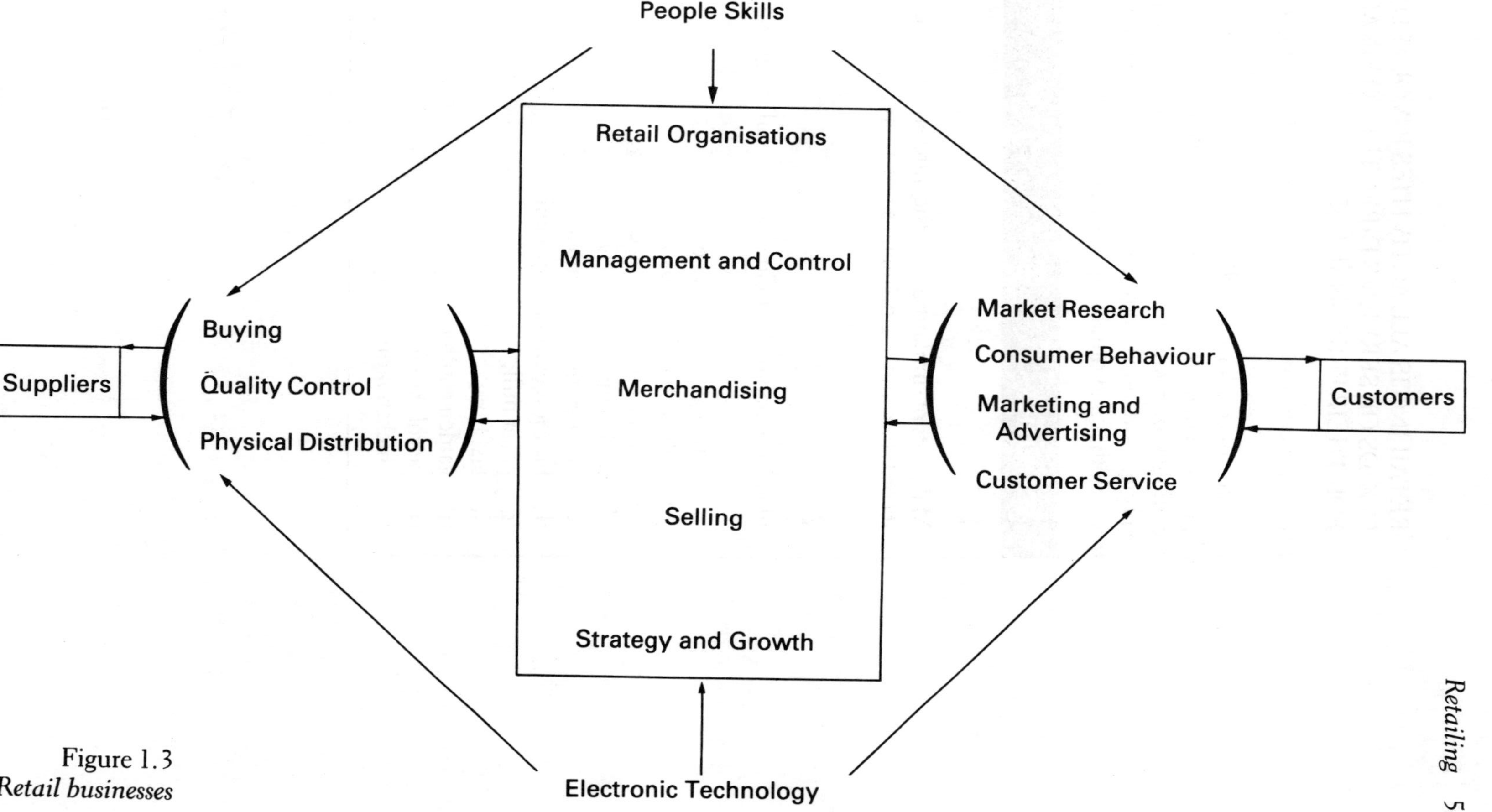

Figure 1.3
Retail businesses

RETAILING IS ALL ACTIVITIES INVOLVED IN SELLING GOODS OR SERVICES DIRECTLY TO FINAL CONSUMERS FOR THEIR PERSONAL USE.

Even so, there is still room for debate. Is, for example, a football league club a retailer? If so, could such a club learn from good practice employed by mainstream retailers? Is a double glazing company who sells some, but not all, of its products to house-owners, a retailer? These questions relate only to the fringes of retail activity, but are posed to emphasise the point that retailing, as defined above, encompasses far more than simply the sale of food, clothes and durable goods from 'shops'.

Activities

1

Make lists of similarities and the differences between an 'Our Price' record store and a McDonald's restaurant.

2

Identify which of the following are retailers, giving your reasons:

(a) catalogue mail order company;
(b) holiday travel company;
(c) mining and quarrying company;
(d) milkman;
(e) office stationery company;
(f) business computer specialists;
(g) paper mill;
(h) taxi firm;
(i) garden centre;
(j) petrol station;
(k) chicken farm.

Unit 2 Buying

Introduction

The buyer is the representative of the retail organisation who is responsible for purchasing goods from the manufacturer or supplier.

With small, independent retailers, the buying function is just one of the many duties carried out by the owner of the shop.

The larger the organisation, however, the more specialised the buying function can be. In Boots, for example, there is a buyer for baby foods. In Sainsburys, there is a buyer for white bread. In Harrods, there is a buyer for 'future presents', such as leather floppy-disc holders!

Centralised buying versus de-centralised buying

If you are on holiday in another part of the UK, and you visit familiar shops, such as Burtons, Top Shop or Boots, you will observe that the range of goods available for sale is very similar (perhaps the same) as those on sale in your home-town branch. The reason is that the retailers concerned have a *centralised* buying department, responsible for buying the goods to be sold at all their shops.

Centralised buying provides a consistent product offer in all multiple retailer's stores and gives shoppers the security of knowing what they can expect to find.

Can you see any other advantages to the retailer of using a centralised buying scheme? What may be the disadvantages of such a system to the retailer and to the shopper?

With a *decentralised* buying system, the responsibility for buying the goods is not entirely given to the head office. Some buying may be done at a regional, or even local (that is, store) level.

Many retailers allow local store managers to make their own choice from all the goods that are available in the central warehouse, and buy seasonal goods, such as fruit, from local suppliers.

Own-label goods versus manufacturers' brands

Own-label goods are those goods with the *retailer's* (rather than manufacturer's) name on the label or packet. If you visit any of the large food retailers – Sainsbury, Tesco, etc. – you will be able to purchase, for example, frozen peas or fruit cordial or toilet rolls or a bottle of wine, sold under the retailer's own label. So, you may see Sainsbury's Garden Peas offered as an alternative to a manufacturer brand such as 'Bird's Eye'; Tesco orange cordial offered as an alternative to 'Robinsons'. The list is endless.

Pay a visit to one of the food retailers listed above. Go to a particular aisle, such as frozen vegetables or wine, and estimate the percentage of display space allocated to own-label goods, as opposed to manufacturer brands.

The exercise should convince you that, for many multiple retailers, own-label goods are a substantial part of the business.

Where do the retailers buy own-label goods? They go, in the main, to the same companies who supply the manufacturers' branded goods. So, it would be quite likely that the retailer's own-label yoghurt, for example, will be sold as an alternative to a branded yoghurt, and both will have been supplied by the same company. The retail buyer will, for the branded yoghurt, negotiate prices, quantities and methods of delivery with the supplier. For the own-label yoghurt, from the same supplier, the buyer will also be involved in the carton and label design, the recipe, the quality control, etc. The retailer's reputation is more directly at stake, and the quality and presentation of the goods becomes part of the buyer's responsibility.

Qualities of a retail buyer

Historically, retail buyers had the reputation (perhaps, deservedly) of being tough and uncompromising, doing their best to squeeze the maximum price concessions from the various suppliers. While negotiation skills for buyers are undoubtedly very important, the relationships between some retailers and their suppliers have become more of a partnership than a battle and, particularly with the advent of own-label goods, the buyer has been required to have a greater understanding of the supply and manufacturing process.

Therefore, the buyer, more than ever, requires skills of dealing with people at all stages of the manufacturing process, a detailed product knowledge, and a commercial awareness, both from a retailing and manufacturing perspective. While the buying and selling prices of the goods are of paramount importance, they may need to be balanced against product quality, or research into new product development, when choosing the best supplier.

Conclusion

Within a retail organisation, the buyer will work closely with colleagues in marketing, finance, store operations and physical distribution, and with specialist technologists in, for example, the areas of fabrics or foods. It is little wonder that retail buyers build up expertise which, in itself, is a great asset to the company, and that the position of retail buyer is highly competitive.

Activities

1

List some of the personal characteristics you would expect a retail buyer to possess.

2

Examine the labels on own-label goods, and the labels on manufacturers' branded food goods in your local food superstore. Compare the prominence, and size, of the retailer's name on the former with that of the manufacturers' names or brands on the latter. What differences do you notice?

Unit 3 Quality Control

Introduction

Manufacturers and retailers take it for granted that the consumer values quality in goods and services. The Swedish furniture retailer IKEA have perhaps the clearest message on quality (see Photo 3.1) and give details of quality control to emphasise their claims on the design and durability of the furniture.

IKEA furniture is tested by the state-subsidized Swedish Furniture Research Institute for quality, durability and ergonomic comfort. (See page 28.) Only furniture that passes every test with flying colours is awarded this symbol, möbelfakta. Learn to recognize the sign. It's your guarantee of Swedish furniture, intelligently designed and rationally built to stand the test of time.

Photo 3.1
(courtesy of IKEA)

Search through newspapers, magazines and catalogues for manufacturers' and retailers' advertisements. Classify the advertisements using the following categories:

Price message
Quality message
'Other' message

How important is the quality message?

What is quality?

The retailer and manufacturer need to take a more precise view of 'quality' than is used by the layman (or by the advertiser!). A useful starting point is the Sale of Goods Act 1979. In Section 14(6) it is stated that goods are of "merchantable quality if they are as fit for the purpose(s) for which goods of that kind are commonly bought as it is reasonable to expect, having regard to any description applied to them, the price (if relevant) and all other relevant circumstances."

An important implication of this Section of the Act is that goods do not have to measure up to an absolute standard of quality, that is, they do not have to be 'perfect'.

The Act recognises that mass-produced goods are not identical. Not every pre-packed bag of potatoes is exactly the same weight. Not every piece of timber cladding is free from knots. It would be reasonable to expect, however, that the bags of potatoes exceed a minimum weight requirement, and that the timber cladding will not have an excessive number of knots.

How can quality be assessed?

To establish *statistical quality control* systems, manufacturers have found it convenient to assess quality by either (or both) of two methods:

(i) by *measurement* – for example, by weight (as with the potatoes), length, strength, diameter, elasticity, etc.
(ii) by (expert) *inspection* – for example, defect counting (as with knots in timber), taste, feel, sound, etc.

With, for example, a roll of wallpaper, both methods of quality assessment may be needed. The strength should be measured to ensure that it is fit for the purpose of paper-hanging, and the pattern should be inspected for flaws.

By frequent selection of samples of the mass-produced goods, and either by measuring or inspecting them, manufacturers can make use of well-established quality control chart procedures to prevent (or detect) machine or operator problems with the production process. By these means they can, for example, be '99.8% confident that 2 metre pieces of timber will have no more than 2 knots'.

It is worth noting here that profitable retail outlets have grown from goods which have been rejected by manufacturers. The Pilkington tiles 'Reject Shop', for example, sells ceramic tiles with hardly noticeable glazing defects or chips, at much reduced prices. Reject Shops for clothes and shoes are successful precisely because customers will accept some (often indiscernible) lowering of quality at a lower price.

Identify the 'Reject' or 'Seconds' shops in your area. What is your opinion on the quality of the goods sold?

Effective Quality Control

It would make little sense to apply Quality Control methods only at the *end* of the manufacturing process, and simply reject the defective items. Quality Control needs to be applied at all stages of the process to minimise the number of defective items. If we extend the process to include the supplier of raw materials at one end, and the retailer at the other, we can identify through the simplified diagram below, some of the Quality Control issues involved with the manufacture and sale of, say, a pad of writing paper to the final consumer.

I	II	III	IV
Raw Materials from Supplier	Manufacturing Process, such as Making Paper	Packaging and Labelling before Despatch	Delivery to Retailer to Sell to Customers

At Stage I, the manufacturer will need to control the quality of the pulp and other raw materials from the supplier. At Stage II, every part of the process, from mixing through to rolling machines, will require quality checks. At Stage III, the sizing, labelling and packaging must be checked before despatch. Finally, the retailer will need to conduct quality checks on the product and its condition – that is, is it clean, dry, torn, etc.?

More and more organisations are moving towards a Quality Management System (QMS), as it is argued that it is wiser to build quality into a product from the design stage, through the production and use stage, than simply to remove defective goods by inspection at the end of the process.

Quality of service

The retailer would include quality of service as part of a QMS. For example, in a retail store, the management may have a set policy on hygiene practices to be followed by counter staff selling unwrapped food. They must:

(i) set standards of hygiene which are no lower than those required by the Food Act – for example, type of cutting boards, utensils, cleaning cloths, period of time between cleaning the counter;
(ii) provide staff training either 'in-house' or at the local Environmental Health Department;
(iii) keep records of which staff have undergone which courses;
(iv) appoint supervisors with a particular responsibility to check the cleanliness of utensils and staff;
(v) keep a record of the time and date of each check, signed by the supervisor, showing what, if anything, was not right.

The same process could be applied to till manning, floor cleaning, fresh food displays and all other aspects of a retail store.

Conclusion

Whatever Quality Control methods are used by manufacturers and retailers, there will always be a subjective or cultural view of quality by the consumer. The organically grown carrot may have an essential quality element for one consumer, but be regarded as a blemished vegetable by another. Without Quality Control systems, however, companies are unlikely to satisfy today's consumer demand.

Activities

1

Choose (i) a food product, (ii) an electrical product and (iii) an item of clothing, and describe how you would determine the quality of each chosen product prior to purchase.

2

List the likely methods of Quality Control required by a fish-and-chip shop owner.

3

Write to a multiple retailer of your choice and ask for details on Quality Control/Management within their organisation. How do these relate to your image of the retailer?

Unit 4 Physical Distribution Management

Introduction

When we walk into a shop we take it for granted that the shelves, counters, racks and rails will all be well stocked with the goods we want to buy. However, getting the right merchandise to the right customer in the right place at the right time is an essential, but often unseen, part of all retail business operations. This process is called 'Physical Distribution Management' and has three inter-related major components, namely:

Transport
Warehousing
Inventory Management and Order Processing

We will look at each of these in turn.

Transport

The movement of products from their point of origin to the shop floor can involve long distances and a variety of forms of transport. For example, a wide variety of fresh foodstuffs is flown or brought by ferry into the UK everyday. The fruit and vegetable range of a typical supermarket might, for example, include bananas from the Windward Isles, grapes from Chile, apples from New Zealand, garlic from the USA, avocados from Israel and mushrooms from Ireland.

Nowadays, most deliveries to shops take place by road transport. While many retail companies run their own distribution services and fleets of lorries, a growing number of specialist transport operators now undertake deliveries for retailers (see Figure 4.1).

Year	*% retail goods delivered by contractors*
1978	11
1985	25
1990	40
1994 (est.)	60

Figure 4.1

Photo 4.1

Specialist operators can respond quickly to market changes and they have often been able to avoid getting involved in strikes and industrial relations problems. They can also accommodate seasonal peaks and troughs in demand and deliveries, and they now provide specialist vehicles for the delivery of frozen and chilled goods, hanging garments and fragile products.

Warehousing

Warehousing involves the storage of goods before they are moved to the shop or store. Traditionally, goods were delivered directly to shops and stores by a large number of suppliers and/or wholesalers and then stored on the premises before being put up on the shop floor. However, many of the UK's major retailers, including Asda, Debenhams, Argos, Sainsbury's, Tesco and Woolworth's, operate a system of centralised warehousing with deliveries being made from manufacturers, suppliers and importers to a large central or regional distribution centre rather than direct to the stores. Each shop or store then receives a single daily delivery from the central warehouse. In 1989, for example, Tesco opened 8 new distribution centres handling all of its product range and closed a number of its smaller depots to leave it with a national network of 19 depots to serve its 370 stores. This policy enables the retailers to maintain greater control over stock levels and stock quality, to release valuable space on the high street for conversion from storage to selling space, to obtain quantity discounts for bulk purchasing, to reduce the loss of stock and to generate improved sales data. These large distribution centres have a floor area of up to 300,000 sq. ft. Goods are received on simple wooden trays or pallets and store orders are picked into and delivered in metal cages. Electrical trucks are used to unload and stack the pallets and to pick and then load and fill the cages for delivery to the stores.

Inventory Management and Order Processing

Inventory (or stock) Management involves deciding when to order and how much to order. At one extreme a retailer does not want to run out of stock, at the other there are the costs of carrying too much stock. The questions 'when?' and 'how much?' are easier to determine for products, like groceries, that have a fairly constant pattern of demand throughout the year than for those like toys, that show marked seasonal fluctuations. Inventory costs include 3 components, namely:

Carrying costs – the cost of rent, rates, energy, handling and interest charges.

Out-of-stock costs – the cost of lost sales because of non-availability.

Procurement costs – the costs of the transport and the administration of supplying goods.

The best inventory level is where the sum of all three costs is at its lowest.

There is also growing interest in 'just in time' distribution systems which involve delivering goods to shops and stores just in time for them to be put on the shelves. The objective here is to minimise inventory levels, but such a system demands frequent transport deliveries and computerised ordering. Order Processing involves finding out a shop's or store's needs, transmitting them to the central distribution centre (or wholesaler), issuing the necessary transport instructions and producing the necessary invoices. Once again, information technology is of vital importance and many stores transmit their orders via small hand-held data capture units. Tesco deliver fast-moving products with a long shelf-life within 24 hours of an order being transmitted.

Conclusion

Physical distribution management is clearly a vital element in retail business operations, and retailers are constantly looking to reduce distribution costs and to improve quality as a means of increasing their competitive advantage. Continuing developments in information technology and computer applications will play a key role in this process. Looking to the future, the rapid transmission of information will be just as important as the transport of goods.

Activities

1

Choose any 3 different food products found in supermarkets and suggest the transport methods and requirements needed to deliver them safely and in good condition to the shelves.

2

Outline the advantages and disadvantages of 'contract' distribution services.

3

A national supermarket chain with stores throughout the UK plans to close its existing 40 distribution depots and undertake deliveries from just 5 large new distribution centres. Study atlas maps of the population distribution and transport networks of the UK and select locations for the 5 new centres. Justify your choice in a 400-word report, illustrated with maps or diagrams.

Unit 5 Merchandising

Introduction

The term 'merchandising' has as many definitions as there are types of retailers, but for the purpose of this book, it will be taken to mean the creation of a selling environment. This may be achieved through:

(i) the choice of 'the mix' of merchandise to be offered to the customer;
(ii) the choice of the amount of space to allocate to different items of merchandise;
(iii) the choice of position, or display of particular products; and,
(iv) the use of another sensory means such as music, touch or smell.

Variety of merchandising methods

All retailers, however small, apply merchandising methods. Take the local greengrocer, for example. Initially, the mix of fruit and vegetables has to be determined, and may be subject to seasonal availability (such as strawberries) and changes in consumer taste (such as the liking for more exotic fruit, for instance, kiwi fruit). The allocation of space, and the positioning of products, will depend on the size of the products, but will nevertheless give the opportunity for an attractive mix of colours, a display of freshness, and so on.

The next time you visit your local butcher, or newsagent, look closely at the range and display of goods, and note the methods which have been used to create a selling environment. Ask yourself why a particular method has been used.

The greengrocer above may have, say, 50–100 product lines. The superstores operated by national multiples, such as Sainsbury's, may have 11,000 or more product lines. The merchandising of such a product range is handled very scientifically. Computer plans giving exact shelf positions and mixes of merchandise are generated at the head office to be implemented by the local store management. On, for example, the shelves for breakfast cereals, 'Kellogg's' Corn Flakes will be displayed adjacent to 'Sainsbury's' Corn Flakes in very specific positions and in very specific quantities. It is known that more sales are made from 'eye-level' shelves, which are within easy customer reach, than from high or low shelves, and the computer plans are designed to reflect this.

Which do you think will be on the eye-level shelves: 'Kellogg's' Corn Flakes, or the retailer's own brand? Why?

Merchandising is just as essential in other forms of retailing, such as catalogue showrooms and mail order.

The catalogue showrooms, such as Argos or Index, have, in the main, very few items on display in the showroom. The showroom is designed essentially for the processing of the payment and the collection of the goods. The merchandising is achieved through the design of the *catalogue*. Argos will, however, be required to make similar merchandising decisions to the store retailer:

- What mix of merchandise? They have chosen, for example, not to offer clothes.
- How much space to allocate to different items? They have chosen to allocate 30 pages to toys in the Spring/Summer catalogue. The allocation is revised in the pre-Christmas Autumn/Winter catalogue.
- How should individual items be displayed and placed? The solariums are pictured (with models enjoying the experience) on a page between body-care products and bathroom accessories.
- How can they use other sensory means? Not at all, so the visual presentation must be both clear and colourful.

Mail order relies entirely on catalogues. A Littlewoods' or Great Universal Stores' catalogue, for example, will offer a range of goods which would otherwise only be available in large department stores. The catalogue provides the only means of creating a selling environment, and is the sole merchandising tool.

Creating a selling environment

Let us concentrate, now, on store retailing.

The (mainly) visual aspects of merchandising start with the external and interior store design. This is very big business for the design companies, and considered to be very important, but expensive, for the retailers. Familiar retail names, such as Top Shop, Burton, Asda, BHS, Dunn and Co, and even Oxfam, have undergone store design changes in recent years, including a change of logo, external signage and colour combinations.

What other stores that you know have changed interior and exterior design? What is the message of the new design?

This is followed by the presentation and accessibility of merchandise *within* the store, including the use of lighting, display features, co-ordination and colours. Logical, adjacent positioning of merchandise can be of great importance as many customers will expect it. The position of paintbrushes in a DIY store would logically be near to the tins of paint, and not in the middle of the plumbing section. Clever use of positioning of merchandise can soften the breaks between product groups. For example, if furniture and garden products have to be displayed on the same floor, garden furniture can be used to merge the two disparate product groups. Also, many stores will offer customer services and will provide other information through signs, directories, etc.

Finally, a special atmosphere may be created through the use of music (such as top 20 songs in a 'young' fashion shop), smell (such as perfumery in a department store, or in-store bakery in a superstore) or touch (such as carpeting in furniture sections), and great care will be taken over the design of dress, or uniform, to be worn by the sales assistants.

Visit all floors of a local department store. List the sensory means of merchandising used in the store. How effective are they?

In creating a selling environment, the larger store retailer will generally wish to:

(i) project a favourable and memorable image of the company;
(ii) persuade the customer to view all (or most) of the merchandise on offer;
(iii) make it easy for customers to find, and purchase, the more profitable lines.

As an example of (i), Asda wish to project the image of a retailer who sells more than just food and groceries. So, in the modern Asda superstores, all customers enter directly into the clothing section to the 'George' range of clothes and must pass through the electrical goods, toys and gardening sections before reaching the food aisles. The fresh produce is the last section in the store, in complete contrast to Sainsbury's or Safeway whose images rely predominantly on the food they sell.

The 'walkways' in department and chain stores are examples of (ii), where customers are encouraged systematically to follow the clearly defined path, rather than view the merchandise in a more random fashion. The placing of key items at eye level is an example of (iii).

Conclusion

Retailers clearly use a variety of methods to create a selling environment, and it is important to appreciate that different methods will suit different retail opportunities.

Activities

1

Visit a large electrical retailer, such as Comet or Curry's, and examine the merchandising methods for:

(i) televisions;
(ii) 'white goods', such as refrigerators, washing machines or cookers.

What differences do you see?

2

The following departments are all situated on the 4th floor of a large department store. The floor is 40m × 60m = 2400 sq. metres, which includes room for walkways.

Using the given information, draw a scale plan of a desirable layout of the 4th floor, justifying your choice.

Department	*Area required (sq. metres)*	*Department*	*Area required (sq. metres)*
Cookware	180	Kitchen accessories	200
Telephones	10	Microwaves	20
Cutlery	100	Glass	180
China	150	Gifts	190
Major electricals	250	Clocks	20
Audio	200	TV	100

3

Examine the clothes section of a mail order catalogue. Outline the advantages and disadvantages of merchandising clothes by catalogue rather than in a store.

Unit 6 Selling

Introduction

All retail businesses aim to sell goods and/or services to their customers but this 'selling process' occurs in a variety of ways. We can make a distinction between selling which takes place in shops and stores and other means of selling.

Selling from shops	*Selling without shops*
Personal service	Mail order
Self-selection	Direct mail
Self-service	Automatic vending
	Party selling
	Door-to-door selling
	Tele-sales

In this Unit we will look at these different approaches to selling.

Personal service

A number of factors help to make a successful salesperson including: (i) personal appearance, (ii) attitude to customer, (iii) selling skills, (iv) good communication skills and (v) product knowledge. One of the first things a customer notices about a salesperson is his or her appearance. So it is important that sales staff are neat, tidy and suitably dressed, and special attention should be given to personal hygiene (such as clean hands, nails and hair).

The salesperson projects the company's image to the customer. A cheerful smile, a helpful attitude and a pleasant personality are vital in helping the customer to feel that he or she is someone special. Good clear communication with the customer is also essential. A successful sales person will also have clear and up-to-date information on the goods that he or she is selling.

Product knowledge can be developed in a number of ways, namely looking carefully at the products and studying their characteristics (for example, textiles usually contain information on fibre content and washing instructions), regular reading of the trade press, keeping a check on the shop's current stock position, and making use of the company's training manuals and video cassettes.

The salesperson must also be aware of the company's policies on cheque and credit card payments, in-store credit cards, alterations, fittings, deliveries and the return of goods. Every customer is different and a good salesperson needs to be able to modify his or her techniques and approach accordingly, but we can identify a number of general stages in the selling process (see Figure 6.1).

1. Approaching the customer	– Each customer should be approached promptly and made to feel welcome
2. Determining the customer's needs	– Sales staff must find out the customer's needs and interests before a sale can be made
3. Presenting the goods	– As a general rule, a salesperson should never present more than three items at the same time, and the characteristics and benefits of each should be demonstrated
4. Overcoming objections	– Good product knowledge can help to overcome a customer's objections, and to direct attention to a similar but alternative item
5. Closing the sale	– A sale should be concluded before the customer starts to lose interest. The goods are wrapped/packed and the customer pays for his/her purchase
6. Additional purchases	– Here the salesperson looks to make a related sale once the first sale is completed. A shirt and tie may be suggested to go with a new suit
7. Goodbye	– The salesperson should thank the customer for his or her custom, and bid him or her goodbye. A customer who leaves with a friendly impression will probably return

Figure 6.1 *Stages in the selling process*

Many years ago, personal selling was the norm in almost all types of shops, but during the past three decades there has been a major move to self-selection and self-service.

Self-selection

Self-selection is now commonplace in most department and variety stores like Marks and Spencer, C&A's, Lewis's and BHS. Here the goods are displayed on racks, fixtures and counters, and customers then take the goods they want to the nearest 'cash point' where they are wrapped and paid for. A limited number of sales assistants are available to answer customers' questions, to give advice and to help deter shoplifters, but customers are generally free to browse without being under any sales pressure.

Self-service

Self-service is now the norm in supermarkets, superstores, small convenience stores and in some retail warehouses. The staff are not trained to sell goods – they are employed to fill the shelves, take payment at the checkouts and to keep the store tidy. However, the essential theme of self-service is that the merchandise *sells itself*. Thus the accent is on the creation of a modern shopping atmosphere and environment which encourages customers to inspect the goods, attractive and colourful displays, focused lighting, a layout which groups similar and related items together, and the selective use of promotions.

Mail order

Catalogue shopping is the most common method of mail order, with catalogues like Kays, Great Universal, Littlewoods and Freemans being common in many households. Mail order offers armchair shopping at home, and customers can usually spread the cost of their purchases over 4–5 months. The retailer does not have the expenses of running a shop, and national (and potentially international) markets can be reached from a single operational centre.

Direct mail

This is a rapidly growing method of selling which involves companies mailing promotional information directly to customers on a regular basis. Goods are then either bought through the post or a reply paid card is returned to the company, requesting further information.

Automatic vending

This is selling from a machine. The customer puts a coin or note into the vending machine which then supplies a product. Over 2.5 million vending machines are used in the UK every day selling, for example, hot and cold drinks, cigarettes, confectionery and contraceptives. Such machines can operate 24 hours per day and require little attention other than re-filling, cleaning and the removal of cash.

Party selling

This is a person acting as an agent for a company and organising a party 'demonstration' in his or her own home for family, neighbours and friends. These guests are then invited to buy some of the goods, and the agent receives either a cash or kind commission payment on all goods sold. Products sold in this way include jewellery, lingerie and some kitchen/household goods.

Door-to-door selling and tele-sales

Here salespeople knock on the customer's door or make a phone call and attempt to make a sale. During the past two decades, door-to-door selling has often received bad publicity because of aggressive and at times misleading sales techniques, but a number of products including cosmetics, encyclopedias and windows are sold in this way. Tele-sales, where the initial approach is made by a telephone call, have now become increasingly important.

Conclusion

Each selling method has its advantages and disadvantages, and most retailers use a number of methods within their retail business. The methods chosen in any situation reflect a desire to provide quality, service and convenience at a profit.

Activities

1

Write the job specification for a salesperson in

(i) a furniture and carpet store;
(ii) the perfume counter in a department store.

2

Outline the advantages and disadvantages of (i) personal selling and (ii) self-service.

3

Undertake a survey of the range of products and services sold from automatic vending machines in your local area, and write a 300-word report on your findings. What are the advantages of this method of selling?

Unit 7 Management and Control

Introduction

Cost control and stock control are both essential for the success of a retail business. They are important for the small independent retailer, but it is the requirement by the national multiples to 'do everything by the book (manual)' which comes as a surprise to new employees who are unaware of the need for systems of control.

- Before reading on, list the costs (apart from the purchase costs of goods to be sold) which a retailer is likely to incur, and rank them in order of how big they are.
- What arc the penalties for having too little stock? Too much stock?

Some common financial terms

All managers need to be aware of the basic financial control terms which are used in the retail context.

Suppose, as a trader, you buy a batch of shirts for £600 and sell them to customers for £1000.

Your SALES = £1000
Your COST of GOODS SOLD = £600
Your GROSS PROFIT =
SALES – COST OF GOODS SOLD = £400

You may be satisfied with the £400 gross profit. Suppose, however, you had bought the shirts for £2000 and sold them for £2400, would you be as satisfied with the same gross profit of £400?

The answer is probably 'no', because your *profitability* is lower. Measures of profitability are usually in the form of ratios or percentages and, in this case, the GROSS PROFIT MARGIN, or simply MARGIN, is appropriate.

$$\text{Gross Profit MARGIN (\%)} = \frac{\text{GROSS PROFIT}}{\text{SALES}} \times 100$$

$$\text{In the first case, MARGIN} = \frac{400}{1000} \times 100 = 40\%$$

$$\text{In the second case, MARGIN} = \frac{400}{2400} \times 100 = 16.7\%$$

The profitability, as measured by margin, is much higher in the first case, as you would expect.

Suppose a store has purchased goods for £180,000 and sells them for £400,000, what is the gross profit and percentage margin?

As an alternative to margin, *mark-up* is sometimes used. The mark-up for an item is 'the selling price – the buying price, expressed as a percentage of the buying price'. So for a single shirt bought for £6 and sold for £10:

$$\text{mark-up} = \frac{4}{6} \times 100 = 66.7\%$$

whereas

$$\text{margin} = \frac{4}{10} \times 100 = 40\%$$

Controlling stocks and costs

Gross profit, as defined above, does not take account of costs such as wages, rent, equipment, energy, etc., which all retail businesses must bear. The sum of these additional costs will be called *expenses*. For this reason

NET PROFIT =
SALES – COST OF GOODS SOLD – EXPENSES

is a more practical measure for retailers. We can see that net profit can be increased by either, or both, of two changes, that is:

(a) an increase in sales value,
(b) a reduction in expenses,

assuming that the purchase cost of goods stays the same.

(a) To increase sales value, the selling price per item can be increased as long as customers will buy at the higher price. Clearly, the selling price cannot be set unrealistically high, and, in practice, many retailers set the price by adding an average percentage mark-up to the purchase cost of the goods.
Another way of increasing sales value in a period is to *sell more goods* in

that period. A useful way of monitoring and controlling the rate of sales of goods is to measure the *stock-turn*:

$$\text{STOCK-TURN (per year)} = \frac{\text{ANNUAL COST OF GOODS SOLD (£)}}{\text{AVERAGE STOCKHOLDING (£)}}$$

If a store has annual sales at cost of £50,000 and the value of the average stock held in the store is £10,000 then the stock-turn = 50,000/10,000 = 5 times a year. If the value of the average stock is £5000, the stock-turn is 10. The higher the stock-turn, the less stock is required to achieve a given level of sales. The less stock, the less is the likelihood of pilferage, damage and perishability of stock, and the greater is the availability of selling space and capital.

With a company such as Safeway which sells mainly food items, stock-turn will be high, but margins will be relatively low. They require high volume sales to achieve high stock-turns and so increase sales and net profits. With a car dealer selling Rolls-Royce cars, stock-turn will be relatively low, but margins will be very high to compensate.

A Department Store sells a wide range of products. Complete the following table, based on your guess of how long things stay on the shelf before they are bought.

Product group	*Stock turn (H = high, M = medium, L = low)*	*Margin (H = high, M = medium, L = low)*
Food	H	L
Electrical	L	H
Men's fashion		
Ladies' fashion		
Bedroom furniture		
Cooking utensils		
Glassware		

The secret of good management is to find an appropriate balance between stock-turn and margin. The management and control of stock depends on the choice of a suitable ordering system. Such a system will guide the retailer as to the order quantity for replenishment goods and the time to place a re-order. Ideally, stock should arrive in the selling area at the time the customer wishes to purchase it. No system as yet can achieve this. Consequently, a balance must be achieved which avoids stock-outs of items (which result in sales losses) and overstocking (which results in high stock-holding costs). The latter problem is acute for small retailers who may quickly encounter 'cash flow' problems. They may have borrowed large amounts of money to pay for stock, and will not be able to repay the loan (and interest) until stock is subsequently sold to the customer.

(b) For a retailer, the major cost elements in 'expenses' are (in order of magnitude):

(i) labour,
(ii) premises,
(iii) transport,
(iv) energy,
(v) stock-holding.

If a company can reduce any of these costs, it has a marked effect on net profit. If £1000 is saved on transport, for example, through use of a more efficient distribution system, the net profit is increased by £1000. A £1000 increase in sales, however, may entail extra labour costs of £600 and will only increase net profit by £400.
More cost-efficient energy provision will reduce heating, lighting, electricity and transport costs. Use of modern technology or an efficient staff scheduling system may reduce labour costs. Retailers will often contest rental increases as they mean direct reductions in net profit. The new uniform business rates worry retailers in case they increase the costs of premises. Concern with costs, and their control, is rightly considered to be an essential management role within a retail organisation, and applications of systems which monitor costs is expected of all managers.
Indeed, some retailers clearly adopt a strategy of cost control. Kwik Save, for example, is well known for keeping a tight control on labour costs, and this is reflected in both their prices and their net profits.

Other areas of management control

When goods which are purchased from the supplier are not ultimately sold to the customer, *'shrinkage'* is said to occur. Shrinkage can take a number of forms. For example, it may be due to poor recording procedures. However, a common cause is pilferage by employees or by customers. Crime prevention, through closed circuit TV systems, store detectives or rigorous employee selection methods, is common practice for large retailers, and is often supported by shopping centre, or store, security staff. Where shrinkage is, say, 5% of the costs of goods sold, any reduction through crime prevention has a positive effect on net profits.

Controls also need to be in place to ensure compliance with the law in areas such as Health and Safety legislation, and that the retailer does not exceed credit limits set by suppliers or financial institutions.

The small retailer

Each area of management control covered in this Unit, and others, is considered important enough by multiple retailers to be a significant part of management training and the associated company systems and manuals. For the small retailer, there may not be a back-up of a company system and it is therefore very important that he or she is aware of the importance of management control and able to seek specialist business training or advice in the area.

Conclusion

Successful retailers must have efficient and effective systems of management and control. Such systems are just as important in small independent businesses as in large multiple organisations.

Activities

1

Draw up a list of the specific cost advantages a chain store retailer may hope to gain by reducing the number of customer pay points.

2

Visit a local, independent, retailer such as a butcher, greengrocer or newsagent, and establish how stock ordering and control is undertaken. How might it differ from the systems adopted by the large national multiples?

3

List the likely sources of shrinkage within a frozen food section of a superstore.

Unit 8 Retail Strategy

Introduction

Small local shopkeepers and superstore managers alike face many daily decisions, for example about ordering fast-moving and slow-moving items, staffing rotas, customer complaints and shoplifting. They also have to take more complex decisions relating, for example, to redesigning the layout of a floor, or how to react to a period of prolonged economic recession and high interest rates. In taking both these types of decisions, retailers are essentially responding to fairly short-term changes, problems and opportunities in their own companies and in their immediate trading environment. However, many retail companies are also concerned to develop a planned and rational view of their long-term goals and objectives. This process is known as retail strategy, and we will look at two particular aspects of strategy, namely growth and positioning, in this Unit. Growth relates to the expansion of a company's business, while positioning concerns the desire to develop a distinct and clearly identifiable position within the overall retail market.

Growth

All retailers are interested in growth, and we can identify 4 general strategies for growth, namely:

(i) diversification,
(ii) geographical expansion,
(iii) merger and acquisition, and
(iv) partnership agreements,

but we should note that an individual retail company may be pursuing all four at any one time.

(i) *Diversification*
Many retailers have looked to achieve growth through changing and expanding their product range and trading operations (see Photo 8.1). During the 1970s, the traditional grocery supermarket groups like Asda began to diversify their product range into household goods. Sometimes, in this process of diversification a new retail format emerges. W. H. Smith, for

Photo 8.1

example, the traditional newsagents and booksellers, moved into DIY retailing with 'DO-IT-ALL' in the 1970s. There is also a growing interest in diversification into the retailing of services. Marks and Spencer introduced their chargecard in the mid 1980s, and it provided the bridgehead for the launch of a unit trust scheme in 1988. In a similar way, Asda had introduced 'Asda Property Services' into 20 of their stores by 1990. They offer a comprehensive service covering surveys, solicitors, mortgages and insurance for anyone buying or selling a house.

(ii) *Geographical expansion*

Growth through geographical expansion is a common theme. Retail companies look to attract new customers and business by opening new shops and stores in areas which they had not served before. The companies who pioneered the introduction of superstores in the 1960s and 1970s illustrate this process very clearly (see Figure 8.1). The first Asda stores, opened in 1965, were all in West Yorkshire, and nearly all the early developments were in the North of England. During the 1970s, the company continued to expand in the North but a number of stores were also opened in Scotland, South Wales, Southern England and the West Midlands. During the 1980s, Asda looked to expand further its network into Southern England, while one of its traditionally Southern-based rivals, J. Sainsbury, was turning its attention to Northern England.

International expansion is also a growing theme. A number of British and European retailers trade in the USA; the British-based Body Shop has

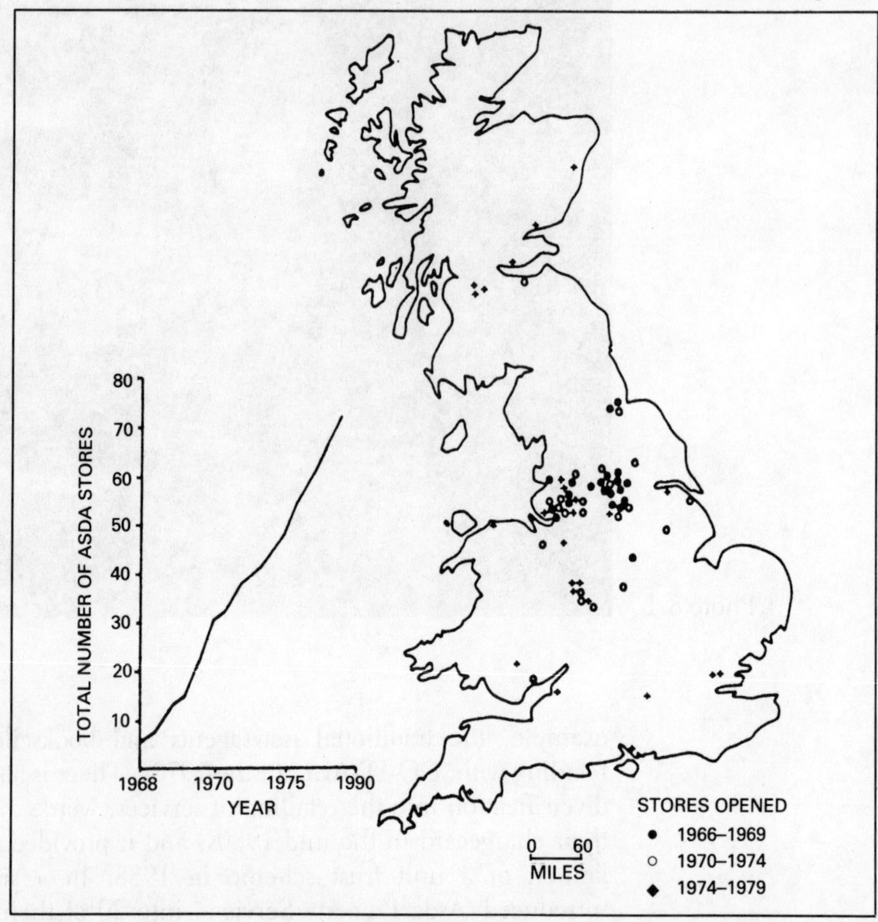

Figure 8.1 *The spread of Asda stores* (source: P. Jones, 'Retail innovation and diffusion: the spread of Asda stores', *AREA*, Vol. 10, No. 3, 1981)

outlets in over 30 countries world-wide and in 1989–1990 Marks and Spencer's overseas sales reached almost £800 million.

(iii) *Merger and acquisition*
Merger and acquisition has been a popular strategy for rapid growth. During the early 1980s, for example, Woolworth's (now part of the Kingfisher Group), a traditional high street retailer, became the largest DIY retail warehouse operator in the UK by acquiring B&Q and Dodge City. Ideally, such merger and acquisition activity should bring together the best of both companies and produce a greater competitive edge, but in practice it has not always proved to be a success. For example, the Asda–MFI acquisition in 1985 did not meet with great success and MFI re-acquired its independence via a management buy-out two years later.

(iv) *Partnerships and joint ventures*
Although retailing is a fiercely competitive business, a number of companies have looked to work together on new projects in a variety of ways. In 1989, Asda entered into a joint venture with the George Davies Partnership which assumed immediate responsibility for clothing and footwear in all Asda stores. Concession counters (such as for perfumes) and separate units (for example, Dorothy Perkins in Debenhams) are particularly common in department stores.

Positioning

Positioning refers to the way in which customers view a retailer in the market place. As retailers look to define and target their customers more clearly, so it is important that the company's retail image specifically appeals to this target group.

Four major factors are said to influence market position, that is:

(i) merchandise (such as range and availability of products);
(ii) customer service (such as product support services);
(iii) trading format (such as location/size of outlets);
(iv) customer communications (such as advertising).

Research suggests that a good image either differentiates a shop or store from its competitors, or positions it close to the general public's view of a model or ideal retailer. Some companies like Marks and Spencer and J. Sainsbury seem to have managed to combine both approaches. A number of elements go to make up a company's retail image, namely:

(i) prices,
(ii) advertising,

(iii) design and shop refurbishment,
(iv) own label products,
(v) quality of service,
(vi) merchandise.

Design, service and merchandising seem to be the most important.

The current research suggests that the more successful a company is in achieving a distinctive position and image, then the more successful its financial and commercial performance will be. At the same time, it is clear that some retailers lack a clear identity and have developed a confused image in customers' minds.

Conclusion

During the past few years, many retailers have developed a co-ordinated approach to strategic planning and thinking. The ultimate aim of such an approach is to create a clear competitive advantage over their rivals which will provide financial success and growth.

Activities

1

List the factors you think major retailers will consider when they look to expanding their business through (i) acquisition and (ii) geographical expansion.

2

Why do you think traditional high street retailers like Boots and W. H. Smith have diversified their retail operations?

3

Hold some brief discussions with your family and friends and try to discover the general image they have of:

(i) a named local superstore,
(ii) a named furniture store,
(iii) Marks and Spencer.

Describe the differences in their images and suggest possible reasons for these differences.

Unit 9 Market Research

Introduction

In the companion book *Markets* in the 'In Business Now' series, the value of market research to businesses in general is explained. For retailers, in particular, market research is undertaken because:

(i) retailers need to be in touch with *consumers* and customers;
(ii) properly selected and interpreted market *information* gives retailers a competitive edge.

Broadly speaking, market research can be classified as

- secondary research (or desk research)
- primary research (or field work)
- group discussions.

Sometimes a combination of all three methods is used, and often retailers will employ specialist market research agencies to conduct the research on their behalf.

Photo 9.1
In-store market research

Typical examples of retail market research activity

Secondary research
A leisure organisation is considering the opening of a new betting shop in a suburb of a large city in the West Midlands. Market research is required to know the size of the local population, and the trends in betting shop usage in the Midlands, prior to making a final decision.

A search for available published data on the particular market can be an effective and cheap use of research time in a context such as this. Information on local population characteristics may be found in published Census data. For market trends it is worth considering, for example, the purchase of a 'Keynote' report on *Betting and Gaming* at a cost of £155 (in 1990).

Primary research
A local, independent, electrical retailer, who specialises in sales of second-hand TVs, video recorders and small audio equipment, wishes to assess the viability of running a video library from the shop. A decision to go ahead with such a venture will have a dramatic effect on the operation of the shop, as the video cassettes will require considerable floor display space (currently used for TVs), and the shop opening hours will have to be extended. Market research is required to assess public demand.

Primary research methods may be employed to:

(i) estimate the number of households, within a 5 minute walking distance, which have a video recorder;
(ii) assess the frequency of video hire of households in the local area;
(iii) determine the views of current customers on the films and other videos which they hire, and where they hire them from;
(iv) examine prices and opening hours of competitors in the local video library market.

Group discussions
A Building Society wishes to 'sell' more financial services to the under 30s, and has decided to use TV advertising to create awareness. It is important that the TV message encourages the young investors, but does not alienate the existing, mainly older, investors. Market research is required to assess consumer reactions to four potential themes for the TV advertising campaign.

The Building Society may organise several discussion groups, each of 8–10 people, and show them the potential advertising themes and scripts. A professional group facilitator will attempt to direct the group members to describe their feelings about the advertisements. Comments such as 'I felt uncomfortable with the advert, because I was being talked down to', if shared by other members of a group of male, under 30s, is valuable information. The possibility that the script will be perceived as patronising and offputting can be further explored.

Conclusion

Market research is, for many retailers, a regular and important element of marketing activity. If it is carried out correctly and efficiently, either in-house or through outside agencies, the information obtained is essential for rational decision-making.

Activities

1

Look in your central public library for local area Census publications. For your town, find the total population, the number of males and females, and the number of under 5 year olds. What other information is given? How might it be of value to a leisure retailer? How up-to-date is the data?

2

Produce a simple questionnaire designed to obtain customer attitudes to shop opening hours in:

(i) town centres,
(ii) neighbourhood shopping area,
(iii) out-of-town retail parks.

Describe how you would use the questionnaire to provide information for a short report on shop opening hours.

Unit 10 Consumer Behaviour

Introduction

It is extremely important for retailers to understand consumers' shopping behaviour.

What factors persuade a consumer to purchase a blouse, for example, at Top Shop rather than BHS? Or vice versa?

What factors persuade a consumer to make the weekly shop at Asda rather than Tesco? Or vice versa?

What factors are considered by a consumer when making a long-term, relatively expensive purchase, such as a new car, which he or she may not consider when making a regular, inexpensive purchase such as toothpaste?

Why are some consumers loyal to a particular brand, such as Kellogg's Corn Flakes, while others will purchase any bargain offer?

What the consumers say

In a recent, TV audience-participation programme on the future of shopping, members of the audience were asked to describe their shopping behaviour. Some of the replies are paraphrased below:

Person A: 'When I go to buy a new skirt, I enjoy spending all day looking at, and comparing the goods in different shops, before I make a purchase.'
Person B: 'I cannot stop myself purchasing special offers and I buy, on impulse, everywhere I go.'
Person C: 'I always make a list for weekly shopping and stick to it.'
Person D: 'I would never purchase goods advertised in direct (junk) mail because I need to see and feel goods which I purchase.'
Person E: 'I hate shopping.'

The responses demonstrate the difficulties with providing universal answers to questions about consumer behaviour.

Try and assess how your friends/colleagues behave when making a purchase of, say, a pair of shoes. For their last pair purchased, list the factors which determined their final choice, and highlight the similarities and differences in their behaviour.

To what extent do you think the purchases were 'planned' or 'on impulse'?

A model of buyer behaviour

P. Kotler, in his book *Marketing Management: Analysis, Planning and Control*, has attempted to provide a model of the decision processes which govern the purchasing behaviour of consumers. The model is summarised in Figure 10.1.

Figure 10.1 *Decision-process model of buying behaviour*

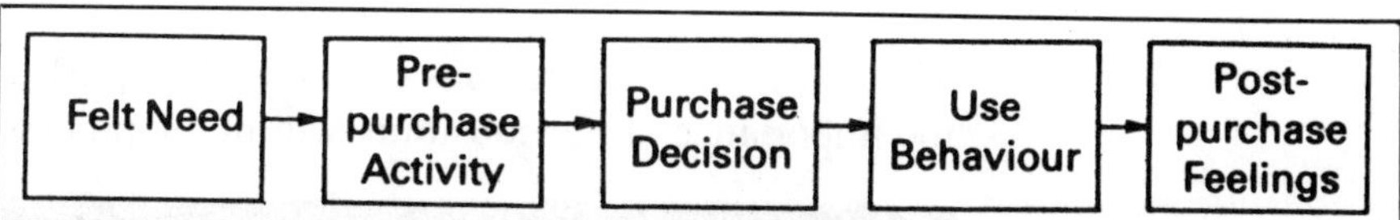

To appreciate Kotler's model, imagine that you are about to embark on a summer holiday. A need is felt for a pair of summer shorts. In the pre-purchase activity, you will search for particular types or brands of product which may satisfy the need. Your actual purchase decision may depend on aspects such as price, style, method of payment, accessibility of retailer, etc., and will require you to evaluate all these factors. Having made the purchase, you may well find uses for the shorts, other than that which generated the original need (the holiday). The post-purchase feelings may determine whether you will buy a similar product again (were you satisfied with it?).

For your last purchase of a pair of shoes, use Kotler's model stage-by-stage to help you understand your buying behaviour.

Does Kotler's model adequately describe the behaviour of Person A above? What about Person B?

The 'why' and 'how' of consumer behaviour

It is often very difficult to explain *why* consumers behave in a particular way when making a purchase. In the area of repeat buying, for example, why does a consumer show loyalty to a particular brand, such as a chocolate bar or a newspaper? Retailers and manufacturers may prefer to concentrate, instead, on describing *how* consumers behave and, having established, for example, that 60% of consumers will repeat-buy a particular brand on a month-by-month basis, they can assess more clearly the impact of an advertising campaign which is designed to entice additional purchasers of the brand.

Impulse buying

One feature of how consumers behave which has had a significant effect on retail operations is that of the *impulse buy*, that is, an unplanned purchase made by the consumer. There are obvious examples of retailers actively encouraging an impulse buy, for example, by putting sweets and magazines next to a supermarket checkout.

Conclusion

This Unit, like the previous one, has attempted to raise your awareness of the importance of the consumer within the process of retailing.

Activities

1

Take the last 3 occasions when you made an impulse (unplanned) purchase. Did the retailer actively encourage you to make the purchase? How?

2

How do the following retailers encourage impulse buying? (a) a petrol station, (b) a book store, (c) a catalogue mail order company, (d) a travel agent, (e) an ice-cream van salesman.

3

Suppose you were to purchase a relatively expensive good such as a portable TV, a personal stereo, or a camera. How would your decision-making behaviour differ as compared with the purchase of, say, a can of drink, or a sandwich?
Does the merchandising of electrical goods recognise the differences?

Unit 11 Marketing and Advertising

Introduction

Retail marketing involves attracting customers, trying to persuade them to maximise their purchases, and building customer satisfaction and company loyalty. There are a number of elements in the retail marketing mix (see Figure 11.1).

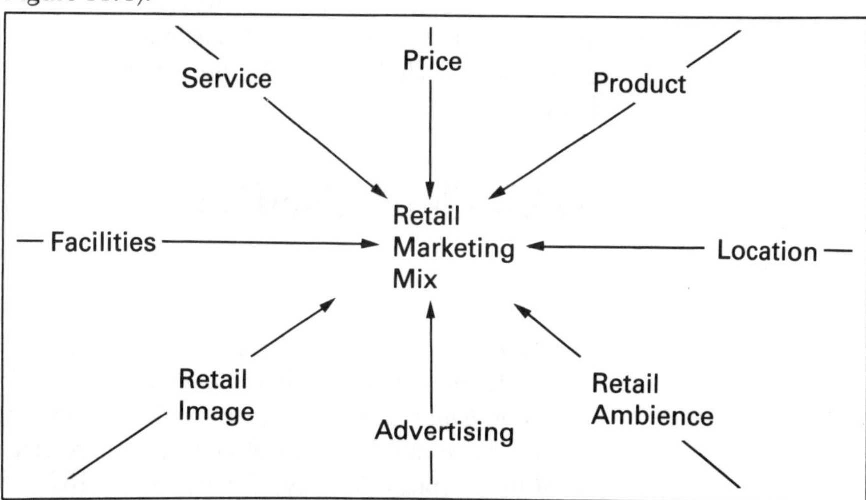

Figure 11.1

Advertising is an integral part of this 'mix' and it plays an essential role in communicating all the other elements to the customer. Retailers represent the largest single group of advertisers, accounting for some 20% of all major advertising expenditure.

Aims and objectives

While retail advertising takes place in a wide variety of ways and uses a wide range of methods, *two* major objectives can be identified:

(i) Promotional advertising – designed to increase the volume of customers;

(ii) Corporate advertising – designed to build the image of the retail company.

Promotional advertising looks to increase customer volume and purchases by advertising particular products, often for a limited period of time, at competitive prices. Corporate advertising has become much more commonplace in the last two decades. Here the accent is upon promoting the image and the reputation of a shop, store or retail company, and upon the establishment of a distinctive position in the retail market place. Two dominant themes are worth looking at: price and quality. The traditional approach was clearly based on 'price', and perhaps epitomised by the early Tesco 'pile it high and sell it cheap' slogan and by the more recent 'Asda price' banner. Nevertheless, a growing emphasis on a 'quality' image can be clearly identified.

This focus on quality embraces service, convenience and variety, as well as value for money. Hence, 'Good food costs less at Sainsbury's' and B&Q's 'Nobody does DIY better'. However, it is important to remember that advertising and publicity campaigns built around a quality theme that is not genuinely reflected in the shop, the service and the products, are a recipe for failure.

Methods of advertising

Retailers use a wide range of advertising methods:

(i) *Television* – TV advertising is expensive but it can hit large audiences at both national and regional level with a powerful message.

(ii) *Newspapers and magazines* – national newspapers and magazines and the large number of local newspapers are extensively used by retailers. On a typical Sunday, for example, 16% of the *Sunday Mirror* is devoted to retailers' adverts. In recent years some retailers, notably J. Sainsbury, have used the Sunday colour supplements to help develop their quality image.

(iii) *Commercial radio* – almost 50% of the UK population regularly tune into commercial radio stations like 'Piccadilly' and 'Capital'. They are a flexible and relatively inexpensive retail advertising medium.

(iv) *Direct mail* – some retailers, both local and national, deliver advertising sheets, newspapers and mini-catalogues to individual households. Such mail often coincides with new store openings.

(v) *The shop as an advertisement* – the retailers' outlets are also very important advertisements for the company. The shop front, window display, interior display, design lighting, promotional material where the goods are on display, carrier bags and most importantly the staff can all be good (or bad!) advertisements for a retailer.

(vi) *Public relations and sponsorship* – a number of retailers use public relations campaigns as well as more direct advertising to promote their image. Marks and Spencer's spent some £4 million on 'community involvement' in 1989 – considerably more than many national retailers spent on media advertising in the same year (see Figure 11.2). J. Sainsbury's staff are actively involved in raising money for national and local charities, the company's home economists visit schools and colleges to talk to young people about healthy eating and nutrition, a number of inner city employment projects have been supported and there is an annual arts sponsorship programme.

(vii) *Customers* – satisfied customers who talk to their friends, neighbours and workmates are perhaps the best advertisement of all. 'If you like us tell your friends, if you don't tell us'.

Figure 11.2 *Major media advertising expenditure by retailers, 1989* (source: Mintel (1990) – *Retail Intelligence*)

DIY Retailers		*Food Retailers*		*Electrical Retailers*	
Company	*£ million*	*Company*	*£ million*	*Company*	*£ million*
B&Q	16.1	Co-op	12.6	Currys	14.4
Texas	13.8	J. Sainsbury	9.6	Dixons	12.4
Do-it-all	6.3	Asda	9.5	Comet	12.0
Magnet	5.9	Tesco	8.1	Rumbelows	6.4
Payless	5.2	Gateway	7.2	Tandy	2.7
Jewson	2.5	Safeway	6.0	Colorvision	2.3
Great Mills	1.4	Iceland	3.9	Visionhire	1.2
Homebase	1.1	Kwik Save	2.6	Laskys	1.0
Dickens	1.1	Morrisons	1.6	Granada	1.0
Fads	0.6	W. Low	0.4	Clydesdale	0.9

Does advertising work?

The old adage says 'It pays to advertise', but is this always true and do some forms of advertising 'pay' better than others?

Some major retailers, like Woolworth's, Littlewoods and the Co-op, have advertised very heavily in the past with very limited subsequent financial success. Conversely, one of the retail successes of the mid 1980s – Next – was launched with an advertising budget of just £140,000.

Marks and Spencer, consistently one of Britain's most successful retailers, spends a very low proportion of their turnover on formal advertising. This suggests that as a growing number of retailers look to stress a quality image, so they may begin to look beyond mass media advertising and to develop their public relations programmes and to integrate them within the overall marketing mix.

Conclusion

The majority of retailers seem likely to continue to commit substantial finances to advertising, but they may extend the methods they employ. At the same time, they will be increasingly keen to monitor their effectiveness.

Activities

1

Study three large advertisements from different retail companies in the local and national newspapers, and write down the main features of each company's advertising message.

2

Outline the advantages and disadvantages of (i) television and (ii) newspaper advertising.

3

Suggest how retailers can develop a favourable image without using conventional advertising.

Unit 12 Electronic Technology

Introduction

Modern electronic technology plays an increasing role in retailing. Three of the most common methods are:

(i) *EPOS (Electronic Point of Sale)*
Through the use of 'scanners' which electronically record the information contained on the 'bar code' of a product, retailers are able, *at point of sale* (that is, the cash desk), to capture data on each item which is sold. Having point-of-sale information accessible for immediate computer analysis has given retailers opportunities for improved management. For example, stock can be controlled by linking orders for replenishment stock of a product line to its actual daily (or hourly) sales.

Knowing *which* items are sold and in *what quantities* will allow retailers to evaluate a sales promotion by comparing sales before, during and after a product price reduction. Knowing *when* items are sold is of value in the planning of staff schedules and determining the peak periods for part-time staff cover.

Imaginative uses of EPOS are forever being found. For example, closed circuit TV cameras can be directed, for security reasons, on those areas of a store which are known to have the largest discrepancies between actual sales and ordered stock.

> Compare the scanning equipment used at the cash desks at Sainsbury's, W. H. Smith and C&A. What differences do you see? Why are some scanners 'fixed' and others in the form of portable 'wands'?

(ii) *EFTPOS (Electronic Funds Transfer at Point of Sale)*
This is a more sophisticated EPOS technology to facilitate the *payment* for goods and services. 'Switch' cards – used in some big stores and supermarkets – enable information to be sent electronically over the EFTPOS network so that the payment is made directly from the customer's to the retailer's bank account.

Only two vouchers – one for the retailer, one for the customer – are required, compared with 3, 4 or 5 part vouchers used with many credit cards.

It is estimated by *Euromonitor* that there will be approximately 600 million UK EFTPOS transactions by 1996, compared with 200 million in 1988.

(iii) *EDI (Electronic Data Interchange)*
Trading, in a conventional way, involves many written communications which are often partly, or wholly, duplicated. The purchase of a car, for example, results in the same 'data' being used for the customer receipt, vehicle licensing, dealer VAT returns, stock adjustments, and so on. EDI is a move towards paperless trading, where data is stored and transmitted electronically. It is of particular interest to retailers in their communications with suppliers.

In addition to cost savings on clerical work and postage, EDI can reduce transaction errors and queries, speed-up deliveries, reduce stock levels and improve customer service.

'Hidden' uses of technology

In less visible or obvious areas, technology has had a dramatic impact on retailing. In the head offices of retail organisations, for example, micro-computers are used extensively for clerical and financial work. Commercial word-processing, spreadsheet and database software packages are established 'tools', while desktop publishing systems and electronic mail systems are beginning to make an impact.

Another example is when a customer applies for a store credit card. Data on the application form gives the retailer both a database and a mailing list. Mrs Norm, aged 48, living in the Home Counties, may be interested in the new winter clothes collection. Why not include details with her next monthly account for her store card? Mr Mod, aged 22, from Sutton Coldfield, may receive, instead, details of the range of compact disc players available in the store. Targeting customers through direct mail is a growing business.

Technology and the 'role' of the retailer

The use of modern electronic technology has made it possible for retailers to identify more clearly what the customer wants, and to respond by supplying it. The goods and services provided by retailers are now seen to relate more to the wishes of the customers, and less to the production methods favoured by the manufacturers. This is seen most clearly in the increased range of drinks and food available in public houses, which for so long were dominated by what the breweries preferred to brew, but are now stocked with a variety of products which reflect the lifestyles and tastes of the drinkers (and eaters). It can be attributed to the emergence of consumer marketing and retail divisions in breweries, supported by EPOS terminals in pubs and restaurants which give them up-to-date sales information.

Case Study: Mrs Field's Cookies

The following Case Study from the USA indicates how information technology can revolutionise retailing.

Mrs Field's Cookies is a 700-store food chain serving the whole of the USA. They have 8,000 employees, but only 6 people in their human resource department. The reason is that the company employ automation at all levels through the use of computerised 'expert systems'.

Every morning, the store managers across the USA switch on their computer and are immediately asked questions such as 'What day of the week?', 'Is it a holiday?', 'Is it a market day?'. They type in answers, the computer compares the information with the last three days which most closely match it, and prints a day planner and labour scheduling program which tells the store manager what cookies to make every 15 minutes, how much batter to mix, and what part-time assistance is required. Each hour, the store manager goes back to the computer and updates it with actual sales information. On a bad day, it may advise on extra selling techniques. On a good day, it will 'up' the estimates.

Their system is intended to give store managers the opportunity to 'drive sales', while letting the computer control the costs. They argue that the computer cannot interact with customers, but can, and should, take care of staff scheduling, production planning, stock control and re-ordering.

Conclusion

New developments in electronic technology can provide major new benefits for suppliers, retailers and consumers, but such developments are often very expensive and retailers will continue to study the costs and benefits closely.

Activities

1

From a small survey of friends and relatives, find out how they prefer to pay for goods and services. By cash? By cheque? By credit card? How might retailers interpret new trends in payment methods with regard to the technology to be employed?

2

Visit your local petrol station. Find out what electronic technology is used, and why. Establish what changes in the use of technology in petrol retailing have been made in the last decade.

3

Write brief notes on the advantages and disadvantages of EPOS.

Unit 13 Customer Service

Introduction

Customers place a high value on the overall level of service they receive. We all hate waiting in a long queue at the bank while eight members of staff sit behind their desks seemingly oblivious to us. A shop assistant who answers our complaint by telling us 'It's nothing to do with me – I was on holiday last week' does little to maintain customer loyalty. Customer service has always been a concern for all retailers, but as competition has increased it has received growing attention.

Range of customer services

In retail businesses the concept of customer service extends well beyond the sale itself. MFI, for example, offer an eight-point fitting service as shown in Figure 13.1.

A number of the food superstore groups offer advice and guidance on food and healthy eating. Sainsbury's have produced a series of free *Living Today* booklets focusing, for example, on 'Your Food and Health' – Does it matter

Photo 13.1

Figure 13.1
MFI complete design and fitting service

Helpful staff always on hand	Friendly advice on planning
High tech design facilities	Free delivery
Expert fitting of units	Install appliances and plumbing
Everything checked by surveyors	The perfect finished look

what you eat?' Try to obtain some of these leaflets and study their 'message'.

Many retailers provide in-store credit cards and discount card schemes. B&Q customers can obtain 10% discount if they pay £25 per year for a discount card while the BHS bronze, silver and gold 'choice' cards offer 5%, 10%, and 15% discount respectively, depending on the amount of money spent in the shop each year. Such credit and discount facilities are seen as an important way of building up customer loyalty. A wide range of other services is offered to customers across the retail spectrum, including clothing alterations, vehicle and roof rack hire, delivery and installation, repairs, insurance, foreign exchange and estate agents.

Customer complaints

While all retailers want to please their customers, complaints can and do occur. Such complaints may relate to goods bought (a hair-dryer may be faulty or a pork pie stale, a dress may be the wrong size or a toy may be damaged), to the service within the shop (queues at the checkout may be long and slow moving, a washing machine may not be delivered when promised or the sales staff may seem more interested in talking to each other rather than in serving customers).

It is essential that complaints are properly handled. Many problems can be resolved by sales assistants or checkout personnel, but some customer complaints must be brought to the attention of the managerial staff. Complaining customers may be annoyed, frustrated and angry, and it is essential that the staff take a patient and sympathetic attitude and get a clear picture of the problem. If the complaint concerns a faulty product, for example, then the customer should be offered a replacement, or if appropriate, a refund. Where a complaint relates to service, then it is important to apologise to the customer and to try to rectify the problem as soon as possible. The best way to reduce complaints is through improved quality control of goods and first-class service, but it will never be possible to satisfy every customer all of the time.

Customer care

The concept of customer care embraces all relationships between customers and the retail company's staff – the objective being to project a very positive image of the company to the customer. A number of major retailers have undertaken customer care programmes (see the Case Study) in an attempt to achieve a competitive advantage over their rivals. The slogans of Asda's 1980's campaign 'Who cares wins' and 'Think customer first' illustrates the central thrust of such programmes. However, the retail staff most likely to have most contact with customers are often among the most poorly paid,

Case Study: 'Hillcare – Making the Difference – First for Customers'

In the late 1980s, the William Hill organisation launched a major customer care campaign. At that time, the company had over 900 high street betting shops throughout the UK and a 8.4% share of the betting shop market. Hill's suggested that customer care could 'make the difference' and give them a major advantage over rivals like Corals and Ladbrokes.

The staff programme was based around some simple but fundamental themes:

What the customer sees	–	Shop image
What the customer sees	–	Personal contact
What the customer hears	–	Personal contact
What the customer hears	–	Telephone contact
What the customer feels	–	Shop ambience

Staff discussed these themes during a weekly programme and were given clear guidelines. The guidelines for the last of the five themes are shown below.

What the customer should feel

- Goodwill promoted with them when they use William Hill
- A welcoming atmosphere when they come into William Hill offices
- Reassurance that visits to a betting shop are acceptable

How is this to be achieved?

- By avoiding personality clashes with customers
- By having a patient and calm outlook at all times
- By looking for the positive side to all situations
- By treating all customers fairly
- By making an effort for the customer
- By treating colleagues fairly to build a team spirit
- By providing that little bit 'extra'

and it is not always easy to convince them to adopt a more positive attitude to their work and to customer relations.

The role of store and departmental managers is clearly crucial in making all members of staff feel they are part of the 'company team'. Many companies use staff incentive schemes to motivate employees.

Conclusion

The customer is the most important person in any retail business – if there are no customers, there is no business. Programmes designed to improve the services, facilities and care offered to customers should thus be an important feature of all retail businesses.

Activities

1

Make a survey of two large stores and write a brief report on the range of services they offer their customers.

2

Imagine you are a salesperson in an electrical shop. You are approached by a very angry customer who shouts at you 'Hey you – that television you sold me yesterday doesn't work'. Describe how you would handle the situation.

3

Give a short presentation to your class on the benefits of introducing a 'Customer Care' campaign in a chosen retail outlet.

Unit 14 Human Resources and People Skills

Introduction

Over two million people work in retailing in the UK. Retail employment is characterised by its diversity. People undertake many different sorts of jobs and duties in a range of different environments. Working hours, conditions and responsibilities vary widely. The head office of a large retail organisation is concerned with overall management, planning and strategy, while the shops and stores actually conduct the business with the customers.

Retail business is also characterised by 'highs' and 'lows'. Some seasons (the run up to Christmas), some days of the week (Saturday) and some times of the day (lunchtime on weekdays) are much busier than others. Thus it is not surprising that some 45% of the retail labour force is part-time, allowing retailers the flexibility to cope with these fluctuations in trade. Some 65% of all retail jobs are held by women and there is evidence of sexual inequality. The average weekly earnings of female sales assistants is just over 70% of that of their male counterparts and, while women outnumber men by almost two to one on the 'shop floor', relatively few of them hold senior managerial positions and directorships. In 1989, for example, only one of the 17 main Board Directors of one of the UK's leading superstore companies was a female.

Other features of retail employment include Saturday (and increasingly Sunday) working, high levels (60%) of staff turnover, particularly in London and the South-east of England, and a substantial recruitment from school leavers who often have no previous work experience.

Human resource management

Human resource management includes recruitment, training, welfare and employment services, appraisal and industrial relations.

(i) *Recruitment*
Recruiting the right people is important at all levels from part-time seasonal sales assistants to graduate entrants and senior managerial appointments.

Marks and Spencer receive 15,000 graduate applications each year; 4,000 of them are called for a first interview, 1,000 get a second two-day interview and 250 receive job offers. In areas like London and the South-east, where there are many job opportunities and staff turnover levels are high, recruitment can be a major headache for large companies.

(ii) *Training*

Many of the UK's major retailers have invested heavily in a wide range of training programmes, including basic induction training for new sales, checkout and backroom staff, continuing training for staff members, a variety of management training schemes and specialised training to meet specific needs and opportunities.

Most major retailers run management training programmes for A-level and graduate entrants. B&Q's 18 month A-level programme introduces trainees to the fundamental disciplines of professional retailing, covering sales floor functions and administrative back-up. Trainees also attend a residential outward-bound course to develop their sense of initiative and team skills. As part of the management team, they play a role in the opening of a new DIY superstore and then spend their last 3 months acting as a departmental manager.

(iii) *Welfare and employment services*

The large retail companies provide a wide range of welfare and employment services to their employees. Such services can include the provision of subsidised living accommodation, medical insurance, sports and social facilities, hairdressing and manicure, administering superannuation schemes, staff discounts, the encouragement of further education and individual counselling on personal and family problems.

(iv) *Appraisal*

Many appraisal systems are employed but the general aim is to assess an employee's performance, attitude and personal attributes against pre-determined standards.

(v) *Industrial relations*

The negotiation of agreements involving pay and working conditions, either via recognised trade unions (such as the Union of Shop, Distributive and Allied Workers – USDAW) or more directly with employees, is also an important element in human resource management.

Interpersonal skills

Working with people is clearly a central feature not only of human resource management but also of retail business. Such skills are often described in general terms as 'getting on well with people'. However, it is possible to identify a number of specific interpersonal skills:

- a smile and a pleasant greeting
- tolerance to other people's points of view
- the ability to listen to what others say
- trying to understand the goals and ideas of people from different backgrounds and geographical regions
- tact and diplomacy
- the ability to motivate fellow workers
- a spirit of interest and enthusiasm
- the ability to work as part of a team.

Conclusion

People – staff and customers – are vital ingredients in all retail businesses. Successful businesses will always need to invest in managing their workforces and in encouraging their workforce to care for customers.

Activities

1

Study four newspaper advertisements for retailing jobs. Describe the main characteristics of each job and of the persons sought to fill them.

2

Prepare your cv (*curriculum vitae*) for an application for a trainee post in a large retail company.

3

Write a brief report on the weekly and seasonal variations in staffing needs in

(i) a large garden centre,
(ii) a toys' superstore,
(iii) a city centre public house.

Unit 15 Retailing in the Future

Introduction

While it is difficult to predict what shopping will be like in 20, 50 or 100 years, it is possible to identify some possible short- and long-term developments within the retail industry.

The changing economic and social environment

A wide variety of economic and social factors may influence shopping. The fear of economic recession and high interest rates will always be a concern of large and small retailers. If retailers look to compete with one another with cheaper prices during times of recession, this will surely lead to the 'survival of the fittest' and to shop closures. Such competition may be fiercest among the grocery superstore groups, and some of today's household names may disappear within the next five years.

Changes in social and population structures will also be important. The growth of a 'younger' retired population with considerable spending power provides major marketing opportunities for retailers, while a lower birth rate will mean a decline in the number of young people in the retail labour market. Social commentators also point to a growing gap between the rich and the poor within British society. In the past, most retailers have concentrated their marketing strategies on the relatively prosperous consumers. In the future, strategies aimed at the less wealthy in society may lead to the growth of a wider range of basic discount shops. The continuing growth in the number of working women will contribute to demands for more relaxed shop trading hours and for increased Sunday trading.

If car ownership continues to increase, then out-of-town shopping developments with good road access and on-site parking will continue to grow. At the same time, there seems to be a growing recognition that improvements in access, parking, and the facilities and environment of town and city centres will allow these traditional shopping areas to 'fight back' and meet the challenge of the new out-of-town developments.

Technology

Developments in technology will surely influence retailing in many ways. Within stores, sales staff may be able to use visual display units to provide instant pictures of how different product styles, colours and layouts will look, allowing customers in a furniture store, for example, to design all the detail of room settings for their own house.

Interactive television could bring tremendous growth in home shopping as people order and pay for a wide range of goods from their armchairs with a remote control. Large weekly or monthly groceries may be then collected at customer pick-up points, while other goods may be delivered direct to the front door. However, it should be remembered that those who also see shopping as a social activity where they meet other people or as a leisure event may not find teleshopping attractive.

Internationalisation

The future seems likely to see a growing internationalisation of retail activity. International expansion may involve mergers, acquisitions and joint ventures, and it may be driven by a desire to compete in large and/or growing overseas markets or realisation that there are only limited opportunities for domestic growth.

Mainland Europe presents the closest expansion opportunity for a number of British retailers. In 1990, Marks and Spencer announced a 5-year programme to open 20 new stores in France at a cost of over £100 million. At the same time, retailers based in Europe will surely cast an envious eye on the high profit margins of British retailers. The possible effects of the creation of a single European market in 1992 on retailers are outlined in Figure 15.1.

Continuing political and economic changes in Eastern Europe and the Soviet Union may encourage retail expansion from more mature capitalist economies. Japanese retailers may also look to emulate their manufacturers and take a much more aggressive view of geographical expansion.

Environmental issues

If more and more people and governments continue to take environmental issues and problems seriously, then this will provide a number of challenges to retailers. Food retailing will perhaps be the first to meet these challenges fully. Here, an increasing emphasis on 'natural' and 'organically grown' products may also be seen as a way of allaying health worries and fears. Certainly many of the UK's grocery superstore chains see 'green issues' as an important element in their marketing strategies, but environmental aware-

1.	Suppliers and buying	Increased power for suppliers and manufacturers Buyers will become more European in their outlook Increased opportunity for importers of products from outside Europe
2.	Physical distribution	Increased speed of cross-border distribution Reduced inventory and transport costs
3.	Regulations	Harmonisation of opening hours Common standards on products (such as food additives, hygiene, labelling) Standardisation of working conditions
4.	Competition	Encourage mergers and acquisition activity Improved openings for North American and Japanese retailers
5.	Consumers	Greater product availability Increase in cross-border shopping More common social values among consumers

Figure 15.1
The effects of 1992 on retailers

ness may extend to many other sectors of the retail economy.

Green initiatives may embrace products, customers and shops themselves. Thus the accent may be increasingly on environmentally benign products, on providing customers with facilities to help them recycle containers and packaging, and on making stores more environment-friendly. Future restrictions on the use of private cars to reduce exhaust emissions and a greater focus on public mass transport could be a major blow to out-of-town shopping, but could help to further revitalise town and city centres. Even more fundamental policies designed to achieve a drastic reduction in levels of resource exploitation and environmental damage could clearly promote a return to a much simpler and more subsistence way of life. This would take retailing back to a simple system of barter for the exchange of essential products.

Conclusion

Whatever the future holds, it will surely bring changes to shops and to the way we shop. As regular customers, we will be able to watch and hopefully benefit from these changes.

Activities

1

Study Figure 15.1 and work in groups to discuss the likely effect of '1992' on British retailers. Make a list of the effects discussed.

2

Design a shopping centre for the year 2000.

3

Make a visit to a large superstore and conduct a simple survey of 'environment-friendly' products.

Index

Acquisition 35
Advertising 35, 43–6
Advertising expenditure 45
Appraisal 56
Argos 19
Asda 34–5
Automatic vending 24–5

Buyer 8
Buyer behaviour 41

Cash flow 30
Catalogue showroom 19
Census data 38, 39
Centralised buying 8
Commercial radio advertising 44
Consumer behaviour 40–2
Consumer Co-operatives 4
Contractual chain 4
Convenience store 3
Cost control 27–30
Costs 27–30
Crime prevention 30
Customer care 52–4
Customer complaints 52
Customer loyalty 51–2
Customer service 35, 48, 51–4

Database 48
De-centralised buying 8
Decision processes 41
Department store 2–3
Design 19, 20
Desk research 37–8
Direct mail 24, 44, 48
Diversification 32–4
Door-to-door selling 25

Economic and social environment 58
EDI (Electronic Data Interchange) 48
EFTPOS (Electronic Funds Transfer at Point of Sale) 47
Electronic technology 47–9, 59
Employment 55
Environmental ('green') issues 59–60
EPOS (Electronic Point of Sale) 47
Expenses 28, 30

Franchising 4

Geographical expansion 34–5
Gross profit 27
Gross profit margin 27–8
Group discussion 37–9
Growth 32–5

Human resource 55–7

IKEA 10
Image 20, 22, 43–4, 53
Impulse buying 41
Independent retailers 4
Industrial relations 56
International expansion 34, 59
Interpersonal skills 56–7
Inventory management 16–17

Joint venture 35
Just-in-time (JIT) 16–17

Kotler, P. 41

Mail order 3, 19, 24
Management & control 4, 27–31
Manufacturers' brands 8
Margin 27–9
Market research 37–9
Marketing 43
Markets 3
Marks & Spencer 2
Merchandise mix 18–19, 35
Merchandising 18–21
Merger 35
Metro Centre 1–2
MFI 51–2
Microcomputers 48
Mrs Field's Cookies 49
Multiple retailers 4

Net profit 28
Newspaper/magazine advertising 44

Order processing 16–17
Own label (brand) goods 8, 18–19

Partnership 35
Part-time staff 55
Party selling 25
People skills 55–7
Personal service 22–3

Physical distribution 14–17
Point of sale 47
Positioning 35–6
Primary research 37–8
Profit 27–8
Profitability 27–8
Public relations 45

Quality 11
Quality control 10–13, 52
Quality management system (QMS) 12
Quality of service 12–13, 36

Recruitment 55
Reject shops 12
Repeat buying 41
Retail buyer 8
Retail strategy 32–5
Retail warehouse 3
Retailing 6
Retailing services 3

Sale of Goods Act 1979 11
Scanners 47
Secondary research 37–8
Seconds shops 12
Self-selection 24
Selling 22–5
Shrinkage 30–1
Single European Market 59
Space allocation 18–19
Speciality store 3
Sponsorship 45
Spreadsheet 48
State-ownership 4
Stock management 16–17
Stock-turn 29
Store card 48
Strategy 32–5
Supermarket 3
Superstore 3
'Switch' cards 47

Tele-sales 25
Teleshopping 59
Television advertising 44
Training 56
Transport 14–15

USDAW 56

Variety of retailing 2–3

Warehousing 16
Welfare 56
William Hill 53–4
Word processing 48